Gallery Books
Editor: Peter Fallon

VENUS AND THE RAIN

Medbh McGuckian

VENUS AND THE RAIN

Revised edition

Gallery Books

This revised edition of
Venus and The Rain
is first published
simultaneously in paperback
and in a clothbound edition
on 30 November 1994.

The Gallery Press
Loughcrew
Oldcastle
County Meath
Ireland

ISBN 1 85235 143 8 (*paperback*)
    1 85235 144 6 (*clothbound*)

The Gallery Press receives financial assistance from An Chomhairle
Ealaíon / The Arts Council, Ireland, and acknowledges also the assis-
tance of The Arts Council of Northern Ireland in the publication of
this book.

Contents

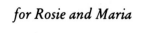

for Rosie and Maria

Venus and the Sun

The scented flames of the sun throw me,
Telling me how to move — I tell them
How to bend the light of shifting stars:
I order their curved wash so the moon
Will not escape, so rocks and seas
Will stretch their elbows under her.

I am the sun's toy — because I go against
The grain I feel the brush of my authority,
Its ripples straying from a star's collapse.
If I travel far enough, and fast enough, I seem
To be at rest, I see my closed life expanding
Through the crimson shells of time.

But the stars are still at large, they fly apart
From each other to a more soulful beginning;
And the sun holds good till it makes a point
Of telling itself to whiten to a traplight —
This emptiness was left from the start; with any choice
I'd double-back to the dullest blue of Mars.

Vanessa's Bower

I will tell you words which you will
Probably soon afterwards throw out of
Your head, where everything is in order,
And in bloom, like the bird-cherry reading
In a frostless climate, or the cheerfulness
Of ships being wooed by the sea away from
My possessive arm. Dear owner, you write,
Don't put me into your pocket, I am not
A willow in your folly-studded garden
Which you hope will weep the right way.
And there are three trains leaving, none
Of which connects me to your E-shaped
Cottage. Alas, I have still the feeling,
Half-fatherly, half-different, we are
Travelling together in the train with this letter,
Though my strange hand will never be your sin.

Ode to a Poetess

1

The rain has left a scare across the countryside;
The air at the bottom of the sky is swimming closely.
What survives of our garden is held together
By the influence of water, as if we could only live
In the shelter of each other, and just leave the matter
Where we must leave all the doors that matter.
How clear and beautiful and hard to bear,
The shutters of these full delaying months,
Like a window not made to open, or a house
That has been too long to let, my dark woman's
Slope. While the noise of the moon is like
Valerian drops when you come into a room
Late at night, or the strangling of a river
To give shape to its fall. Half-real, half-dreamed,
Untouched, untouchable, the yet-to-be-born weather,
Distempering me as lips disturb the vespered worlds
Of grapes, this onset of a poetess and her
Persuasive bones sending me and my life away.

2

I will not write her name although I know it,
With the never-to-be-repeated awakening
Of a letter's morning freshness, or the wide-
Apart windows I recall of the summers of love,
Where my scholar's fingers bungled their role.
Now you are in a poem of your own cold
Making, on your second fret, your life knit
Like a bird's, when amid the singing
Of the Sparrow Hills you yourself could not sing.
It is ten o'clock, I am thinking of those

Eyes of yours as of something just alighted
On the earth, the why that had to be in them.
What they ask of women is less their bed,
Or an hour between two trains, than to be almost gone,
Like the moon that turns her pages day by day,
Letting the sunrise weigh up, not what they have seen,
But the light in which the garden, pressing out into
The landscape, drew it all the more into its heart.

The Difficult Age

He could not leave his own voice alone:
He took it apart, he undressed it,
I suppose the way that women clear their faces,
So that some light is still able to love them.

He had pushed his voice up from his chest
Into his head until the air from his lungs
Was felt between the eyes. I heard
Those curiously distorted flicks of sound

Like an English choirboy or coherent father,
Or the faraway splash of a brief and dowdy
Bird, turning over its final twenty-second held
Note. I would bid my memory be emotionless

As the second in which his studied lateness
Summoned up an image of sheltered orchids,
Guarding in their permanent white premonitions.
Such easy words as 'Je ne suis pas heureuse'.

To the Nightingale

I remember our first night in this grey
And paunchy house: you were still slightly
In love with me, and dreamed of having
A grown son, your body in the semi-gloom
Turning my dead layers into something
Resembling a rhyme. That smart and
Cheerful rain almost beat the hearing
Out of me, and yet I heard my name
Pronounced in a whisper as a June day
Will force itself into every room.

To the nightingale it made no difference
Of course, that you tossed about an hour,
Two hours, till what was left of your future
Began; nor to the moon that nearly rotted,
Like the twenty-first century growing
Its grass through me; but became in the end,
While you were still asleep, a morning
Where I saw our neighbours' mirabelle
Bent over our hedge, and its trespassing
Fruit, unacknowledged as our own.

From the Dressing-Room

Left to itself, they say, every foetus
Would turn female, staving in, nature
Siding then with the enemy that
Delicately mixes up genders. This
Is an absence I have passionately sought,
Brightening nevertheless my poet's attic
With my steady hands, calling him my blue
Lizard till his moans might be heard
At the far end of the garden. For I like
His ways, he's light on his feet and does
Not break anything, puts his entire soul
Into bringing me a glass of water.

I can take anything now, even his being
Away, for it always seems to me his
Writing is for me, as I walk springless
From the dressing-room in a sisterly
Length of flesh-coloured silk. Oh there
Are moments when you think you can
Give notice in a jolly, wifely tone,
Tossing off a very last and sunsetty
Letter of farewell, with strict injunctions
To be careful to procure his own lodgings,
That my good little room is lockable,
But shivery, I recover at the mere
Sight of him propping up my pillow.

The Sitting

My half-sister comes to me to be painted:
She is posing furtively, like a letter being
Pushed under a door, making a tunnel with her
Hands over her dull-rose dress. Yet her coppery
Head is as bright as a net of lemons. I am
Painting it hair by hair as if she had not
Disowned it, or forsaken those unsparkling
Eyes as blue may be sifted from the surface
Of a cloud; and she questions my brisk
Brushwork, the note of positive red
In the kissed mouth I have given her,
As a woman's touch makes curtains blossom
Permanently in a house: she calls it
Wishfulness, the failure of the tampering rain
To go right into the mountain, she prefers
My sea-studies, and will not sit for me
Again, something half-opened, rarer
Than railroads, a soiled red-letter day.

On Not Being Your Lover

Your eyes were ever brown, the colour
Of time's submissiveness. Love nerves
Or a heart beat in their world of
Privilege. I had not yet kissed you
On the mouth.

But I would not say, in my un-freedom
I had weakly drifted there, like the
Bone-deep blue that visits and decants
The eyes of our children:

How warm and well-spaced their dreams
You can tell from the sleep-late mornings
Taken out of my face! Each lighted
Window shows me cardiganed, more desolate
Than the garden, and more hallowed
Than the hinge of the brass-studded
Door that we close, and no one opens,
That we open and no one closes.

In a far-flung, too young part,
I remembered all your slender but
Persistent volume said, friendly, complex
As the needs of your new and childfree girl.

Epithalamium

Had her hair been a thought browner,
The raisin-coloured hood of love would
Not have seemed so handsome, such a
Dark foil.

A hard blue dress, gutted of its girl
And off-the-shoulder, brought
Half the sky but musicless
Into the evolution of white.

Yet undiluted gold was the mellow
Theory of the poetry of the time, and
Where guilt cuddles us with stranger
Tensions, the rest of the body feels
Very left out.

Your childhood must have been standing
On its head, when you said 'Don't
Call me darling' — that empty, spear-shaped
Word, like a disorder in desire
Which is in fact a loving-in-return:
You know the moon has had
That conscious, fuscous tint all winter.

Scattering

for Hazel

If you had walked in, the room
Would have broken up into questions,
About bedding-out, and whether it is
True to say that such-and-such a pear
Only succeeds against a wall or, if trans-
Planted, is no longer nourished
By its old bad-tempered roots.

For in one minute the moon
Can move the distance of her body,
With all the calm of a pietà,
From a mouth that matches hers, so that
A state of good repair still clings
To Venus putting on her sandals
Abstemiously in the pre-dawn hours.

Perhaps she purchased, by this biblical
Appliqué, less a genuine daylight
Than the aplomb of those winter-white insets
On my edge-to-edge bolero — every one
The logical neighbour of the next — until
The drawstring, like an ordinary mountain,
Scatters its desired and dark effect.

The Villain

This house is the shell of a perfect marriage
Someone has dug out completely; so its mind
Is somewhere above its body, and its body
Stumbles after its voice like a man who needs
A woman for every book. When you put your
Handkerchief to your lips and turned away from
Me, I saw in the lawn that least wished itself
Known the reverse of green fingers, taking an
Over-long walk. Once with your velvet side you
Said you would like to beget a child to look
Out of every window with his own daytime eyes:
Somewhere there's the right colour for this my
Brownest, tethered room, the unloved villain
The younger year may locate, and take into its own.

Painter and Poet

I turned his room into a shell
With the same choosiness that was icing me
All over. I choked the crimson flock
Wallpaper with sheets of mimosa,
That he might be remembered for a handful
Of love poems. Still it was
The warmest room in the house, and he would say
'The closeness of my room never injured me,'
Whenever we had a thunderstorm to ourselves.

Yet some exactness about the posture
Of the chairs would make me foam
Against the beautiful moist heat that could
Bring peaches to perfection on its own,
Without so much as a hint
That their bindings were as constant
As an interregnum in the rain.

Unallegorically, I wanted his quenched eyes
To feel as well as see how the moon and we
Do not amalgamate, and so I mushroomed
The hills of his ceiling into a kind of chapter
Of hats and walking shoes. I cannot say
Precisely 'Perdidi diem', though I dined
Superficially his normal, lovely, melancholic
Wife. For that evening, he scratched out
Regiments of flowers, and went with me
Some distance from the house, perhaps
An English mile, until even
The ghosts of paths were out of sight.

Moonshots

Young ice is going to and fro
Under my hedge of snow; and if
You stumble into me as a great meal,
You may learn how cold a man will feel
In the interior of the moon.

Yet I hold you fast there, your
Rudimentary impression of leaves and stalks,
Like the spin of false suns, or
The doubtful weight of morning,
Preparing to sail away again.

Aviary

Well may you question the degree of falsehood
In my round-the-house men's clothes, when I seem
Cloaked for a journey, after just relearning to walk,
Or turning a swarthy aspect like a cache-
Enfant against all men. Some patterns have
A very long repeat, and this includes a rose
Which has much in common with the rose
In your drawing, where you somehow put the garden
To rights. You call me aspen, tree of the woman's
Tongue, but if my longer and longer sentences
Prove me wholly female, I'd be persimmon,
And good kindling, to us both.
Remember
The overexcitement of mirrors, with their archways
Lending depth, until my compact selvedge
Frisks into a picot-edged valance, some
Swiss-fronted little shop? All this is as it
Should be, the disguise until those clear red
Bands of summerwood accommodate next
Winter's tardy ghost, your difficult daughter.

I can hear already in my chambered pith
The hammers of pianos, their fastigiate notes
Arranging a fine sightscreen for my nectary,
My trustful mop. And if you feel uncertain
Whether pendent foliage mitigates the damage
Done by snow, yet any wild bird would envy you
This aviary, whenever you free all the birds in me.

Isba Song

Beyond the edge of the desk, the Victorian dark
Inhabits childhood, youth-seeking, death-seeking,
Bringing almost too much meaning to my life,
Who might have been content with one storey
And the turned-outwards windows of the isba.*
Its mournful locus, I sit like a horse chosen
For its strength, requiring to be renamed
'Monplaisir', with my two hands free. I have heard
In it the sound of another woman's voice,
Which I believed was the sound of my own,
The sound the first-timeness of things we remember
Must make inside. And although she was eager
To divide her song, from her I took nothing
But the first syllable of her name, so the effect
Was of a gentler terrain within a wilder one,
High-lying, hard, as wood might learn to understand
The borrowings of water, or pottery capitulate
Its dry colours. Otherwise I might have well
Ignored the ground that shone for me, that did enough
To make itself rebound from me, out of which I was made.

*Isba: Russian one-storey dwelling.

26

Harvest

I have taken you for granted like a house,
The harvest of your soft, stone smile. I have
Made you come with me to smell, with your
Winter beard, the treasure of the most sinful
Oceans; or left you lunching at a Russian
Hour, so that you might find my poem
Wrinkled under your plate, like a beautiful
Season you could never be prepared for.

I am the sky of a long day, working
Out its twilight — how to make that steadily
Impulsive blue taper off its solemn
Rind, to fall like a sea-poem in shreds
Between your fingers. Your hand takes it
With the strange whiteness prisoners let grow
Over themselves, remembering the Florentine
Light of restaurants, mourning their tables of rice.

Without ever saying to me you are tired
Of the art of raining, with its oh-so-masculine
Kisses, and the way it draws its suicidal
Bloom across the wall like a huge long
Painting of the sea. As if some blue god
Denied September opening her doors so wide,
His sharp sound unanimous lest
Twilight and I come at the same time.

Freeze-Up

The change in your voice when speaking
Is like an orange in a snowdrift, the warmth
Of its pocket. I shall no longer now be dark
In your mind, though I still shade you
From life elsewhere, as the glass continues
Coping with things that have passed, not
Always between us.
                        Whiskers of moonlight
Raise the grass to the distinction of a normal
Beach, yet our lost harvests hang in the moon's
Sky like ambassadors of cold, staining
That fair-weather world until she thinks
Herself a poor snowmaker, erring on the side
Of melting.
                        Even the sea has its own
Calamities, memories of the chill of long ago
When some peculiar stirring in the sun
Made fashionable imaginary summers
After a winter three winters old.
                                        And such
A sharp line is this, the wettest part of the storm
Would not be moved by the sight of soil
Blowing away in the wind, nor the forest,
Conscious how a desert grows from brightness,
Follow the deepest, quietest-spoken cloud.

The Hard Summer

Then I was one long curve, from
The top of my head to my toes,
And an unseen arm kept me from
Falling over. My locked line
Was a kind of sweep, like the letter
S, diffusing as it pulled away
The light that came from below.
Your fingers found how breast
And arm change when they press
Together, how the bent leg
Hides even from the married
The *H* behind the knee. Though
Certain bones lie always
Next to the skin, an elbow
Forcing the back to crease
Might just be playing 'The Hard
Summer' for us, like a gift
That passes from father to daughter.
All that is month-named is
The *T*-shape of your face in the
Spring shadows, folds in your palm
That fall aside like breasts,
Creating the letter *M*.

Prie-Dieu

Although my dresser still contains
Christmas cards in May, I have ceased
To send the bluebelled notelets mourning
The world that is dead in me, my mother's
Sleeping-hide. It seems at last
My upright chair beside a separate
Fireplace can cope as well
As any honest woman with the rage
Of one moment, the contentment of the next.

You see me all untutored, always
Sexed, a postulant that will not kiss
Until the clothing ceremony. Yet
This oblique trance is my natural
Way of speaking, I have jilted
All the foursquare houses, and
My courtyard has a Spanish air,
Defiant as a tomboy. Under the pelmet
And the reading lamp, the white
St Joseph, a bunch of flowers
Clearly gathered by a child.

Waters

In quiet streams, the buoyancy of water-lily leaves
Will take the even weight of a child on their celled floors;
The bamboo dies as soon as it has flowered, however scantily;
The sacred lotus opens wide on four successive nights.

A search round fern patches in the autumn will discern
A ribbon or a heart of simple moss that hugs the ground
Where spores have fallen — some have changed their leaves
To roots, and left the shore for the eternal spray of waterfalls.

Straw-coloured rhododendron trusses seem insensible
To snow, with their felted backs, of tan or silver brown:
The barrel-palm appreciates above its swollen trunk
The neat habits of camellias, the water-loss of dates.

Venus and the Rain

White on white, I can never be viewed
Against a heavy sky — my gibbous voice
Passes from leaf to leaf, retelling the story
Of its own provocative fractures, till
Their facing coasts might almost fill each other
And they ask me in reply if I've
Decided to stop trying to make diamonds.

On one occasion I rang like a bell
For a whole month, promising their torn edges
The birth of a new ocean (as all of us
Who have hollow bodies tend to do at times).
What clues to distance could they have,
So self-excited by my sagging sea,
Widening ten times faster than it really did?

Whatever rivers sawed their present lairs
Through my lightest, still-warm rocks,
I told them they were only giving up
A sun for sun, that cruising moonships find
Those icy domes relaxing, when they take her
Rind to pieces, and a waterfall
Unstitching itself down the front stairs.

The Prince of Parallelograms

Light circled each side of the river
Like mouths into which grapes were pressed:
A necklace sensationally broken
I associate with her nearness,
Who, denied her own dreams
So she could enter
The stainless dreams of others,
Was chiefly charmed by those
Of her metaphysical child.
More than him she feared
To sleep in a motionless bed,
So she measured down beside me
Like a boatswain.

Rowing

There are two kinds of light, one perfect
Inside, pear-coloured, shedding that cool
Classical remorse over the angered field,
The other gifted with an artlessness too
Painful to live with, like a spur
Eloping from the room below, its nurtured
Discipline of dark tobacco golds. Just
From watching how these circles call
Towards each other, fitfully, whole-
Heartedly, across the slightly
Parted sky, recalls to me the egging tide
That could not parallel its distant
Claim upon the beach, the broken
Line it had created earlier.

What speed compared to my bad rowing
Your body renovates me like an artisan,
A goldsmith, none too delicate, despite
Its strength of loving that with one blow
Might start a blizzard. Austerely as
A backless dress, I fall in with the nature
Of a gleam, a place that is not a place,
Or not the house of my dreams. Where
My hand is, there is the pain that wires
Its sour honey through my flush,
As an ear-ring grows precocious in the vellum
Of a head, with all its sutures
In the offing, or the sand unhindered
Thickening with marble dust.

Artemisia

For six months, one jasmine
Has perfumed my bed — in the morning
It is like the scent of friends, the society
Of roses! Yet I'm learning
How heart odours cling to any wrist
That has lingered over violets
Or immersed itself in musk four-fingers
Long, and spared no alcove
Of the body from its ample mist or rain.
When I accuse myself again of lacking
Water, or that subtle Greek custom
Of disfavouring my older, chosen sachet,
Wearing peachwood, or fenugreek, the artemisia
Offers me the formula of a flower still on stem,
Cupped to the last adulterous perfection.

The Rising Out

My dream sister has gone into my blood
To kill the poet in me before Easter. Such
A tender visit, when I move my palaces,
The roots of my shadow almost split in two,
Like the heartbeat of my own child, a little
Blue crocus in the middle of a book, or the hesitant
Beginning of a song I knew, a stone-song
Too small for me, awaiting a drier music.

She gentles me by passing weatherly remarks
That hover over my skin with an expectant summer
Irony, soliloquies that rise out of sleep,
And quite enjoy saying, 'Rather a poor year'.
I continue meanwhile working on my arm-long
'Venus Tying the Wings of Love', hoping
She will recede with all my heroes, dark
Or fair, if my body can hold her bone to term.

For any that I loved, it was for their hair
That never really belonged to them, its colour
Like a line of clouds just about to crumble,
The breaking of ice in a jar. In my mind,
I try and try to separate one Alice
From the other, by their manner of moving,
The familiar closing of the unseen room,
The importunate rhythm of flowers.

If she had died suddenly I would have heard
Blood stretched on the frame, though her dream
Is the same seed that lifted me out of my clothes
And carried me till it saw itself as fruit.

Hotel

I think the detectable difference
Between winter and summer is a damsel
Who requires saving, a heroine half-
Asleep and measurably able to hear
But hard to see, like the spaces
Between the birds when I turn
Back to the sky for another empty feeling.

I would bestow on her a name
With a hundred meanings, all of them
Secret, going their own way, as surely
As the silvery mosaic of the previous
Week, building itself a sort of hotel
In her voice, to be used whenever
The tale was ruthlessly retold.

And let her learn from the sky, which was
Clever and quiet, the rain for its suddenness,
That yes on its own can be a sign for silence,
Even from that all-too-inviting mouth.

The Thursdayer

My auburn-bearded anxieté du soir —
Look at the little slave legs
Tucked under a chair
Of a girl who in a burberry
Hurried to meet her first shaved statue.

It was she who received
The now unread smile-marks
That woke me stupid from my sulk;
And moved around lightly,
Touching flowers or pushing breakables
A fraction of an inch this way or that,
To be my servant Mrs Peach, Mrs Honey,
Mrs Buttercup.

As soon as she came down
We were a candle in the valiance
Of half-way up the stairs,
Where her room lay tallowy and true.

For the Previous Owner

Now autumn brushes with her lips
The coarseness of flowers that sunned themselves
In the bureaucratic hours, I bring
A certain small wardrobe to the leaf-filled
Light. Its evening scent is from the curves
Of my lilac walking costume, like that
Of a day-late Valentine, or moon-omens
Explaining away the dark hair of the beloved.

Sheaths so immune to the several atmospheres
Of your perfectly positioned body, when I
Turn back the hood I can see the baby's
Breath; while the freed doubt awakens
All the room's shortcomings, its
Inefficient joins, like old-style
Petals with their round faces
Molesting the pendulous wind.

So the weather of your leaving changes
Little, any more than an amanuensis
Dare enhance the Prussian blue you
Set the sea to. If a woman's
Stiffness after labour made way for persons
Who never were, then I would sleep for you,
Your last mutation, though no one can sleep
For you, and no one could renew the blossom
Mouth who bit her own sea-lashed lips.

Dovecote

I built my dovecote all from the same tree
To supplement the winter, and its wood
So widely ringed, alive with knots, reminded me
How a bow unstrung returns again to straight,
How seldom compound bows are truly sweet.

It's like being in a cloud that never rains,
The way they rise above the storm, and sleep
So bird-white in the sky, like day-old
Infant roses, little unambitious roads,
Islands not defecting, wanting to be rescued.

Since I liked their manners better than
The summer, I kept leaning to the boat-shaped
Spirit of my house, whose every room
Gives on to a garden, or a sea that knows
You cannot reproduce in your own shade.

Even to the wood of my sunflower chest,
Or my kimono rack, I owed no older debt
Than to the obligatory palette of the rain
That brought the soil back into tension on my slope
And the sea in, making me an island once again.

Pain Tells You What to Wear

Once you have seen a crocus in the act
Of giving way to the night, your life
No longer lives you, from now on
Your later is too late. Rain time
And sun time, that red and gold sickness
Is like two hands covering your face —
It hardly matters if a whole summer
Is ruined by a crumpled piece of paper
Or the dry snap of a suitcase closing.

Of all silences, the hardest to bear
Is the strange vegetation of your clothes,
A brand-new sleeve becoming haggard
With a garden's thousand adjoining moods.
To make such overperfumed wood speak
A forest language, one must not remember
The mahogany secrecy of eyes once velvet-dark,
Now water-pale — the special lighting
Of their insolent lying there.

Fear of retouching is the very last
Quality suggested by the flag-red,
Flag-gold, storming flowers that,
Without being seen, like one dissatisfied
With his sirings, reach out through winged
Garments to the priceless vertebrae of the stars.

Mad River

September was like one of those persons
With whom you sit and become a lie
(Setting a moral table, making a moral bed).
September was responsible for everything falling
Into moral pleats, and for the childhood
You would have had if your parents had
Described it.

Their first married months were a cave
Of grievances nothing of you ever dented.
His shelves of river driftwood made one solid
Wall of books — his brain simmered so fast
That different parts of the house stopped
In another dance. It was for him she worked
To shift the focus away from herself, lest
Some anxiety bleed into his excitement, or in order
That a little more or a little less light
Might leave him happier.

When she had no more walk to throw away,
Within and without you were the home
She carried. When she was as old
As a town, and rain washed away
The excesses of April, like the effect
Of storms on our bodies, she was reafforested,
For some hours she was young.

Confinement

Child in the centre of the dark parquet,
Sleepy, glassed-in child, my fair copy,
While you were sailing your boat in the bay,
I saw you pass along the terrace twice,
Flying in the same direction as the epidemic
Of leaves in the hall. Our half-unpeopled
Household, convalescent from the summer's leap,
That indiscreetly drew the damp from walls,
And coaxed our neighbour, the forest, into this
Sorority, how could I share with you, unpruned
And woebegone? A swan bearing your shape
Re-entered the river imagery of my arms.

Another Son

The sickly summer draped itself
Against the door like a yard child,
Then climbed into me, pushing back
My sleep earlier than spring. Being
Maimed and overgifted, we were never
As compatible as Browning's troubled
Trochees to the house of salutation,
Or Raphael's unpunished, most serene
Madonna. Nor did I dream how sensitive
My table was, till less and less
Its shadow came to mean the time
Not actually midnight, but a February
Trance whose rigid snow chose coolly
To be homesick for a street it would
Never know; as if we draw on burdens
With a lap child's sense of chairs.

The Return of Helen

Being stored inside like someone's suffering,
Each piece of furniture now begins
To interpret every eye as sunlight;
And that smallness in me which does not vibrate
Is moving nonetheless towards
The white and unworked wool of the corded bed.

The old year in his mimic death
Is my husband like a child unlooked-for
Moistening the wrong turnings I make
Myself take, till the path into my body
And out of it again is a sea-place
Opening where you least expect.

As from an irresponsible
Brood of ten, my love of twenty years
Might oversweetly part your fingers
To count the points, telling why you ravish her.

Star

The ancient river underneath our house
Gives it that intimate malaise, those proud-flesh
Cornices I savour most during their abdication,
Comparing it unfavourably with how the move,
Protracted as it was, killed my only Star
Of Bethlehem. I thought then it might have slept
Warm as the baby through the clatter, or sustained
The diffuse arousal likely from the hands
Of several men. But knowing now how they bruise
At the slightest fit of kindness, I would always
Be expecting it to happen again, however vigilant
My witness. When the wine of me rises very
Strong towards you, I make a show of going out
Under my own manless law, to save me
Going over to your camp. Where you were never
Anything but gentle, never dreamt of girls
In cool colours, starlets docile and distressed,
To break the day for you, the weapons of the weak.

Apricot Ranch

Dissolute leaves have become
The oath on my lips. In the mirror
Forming the backrest of my bed,
There is hardly a word that looks
Forward.

As if when the house changed hands,
So did the ghost,
Or when I poured that glass
Of heated wine into the shrub bowl,
I shed most of my tranquillity
Upon the favoured flowers.

The wedge-shaped room compressing
Me and stretching me, I felt
Something move out of me,
Something that had been waiting there
Always. And imagined the new bones
Of a child in my arms.

My inward, downward glance
Was the illusion of countryside corn
In the garden, after which I probably
Never opened my eyes again.

Felicia's Café

Darkness falls short by an hour
Of this summer's inhibitions:
Only the cold carpet
That owns a kind of flower
Feeds any farm or ocean
Around the bedroom's heart.

Each day of brown perfection
May be colour enough for bees:
The part of my eye
That is not golden sees.

Lime Trees in Winter, Retouched

Black is my continuum, my black wheat ripens
From peach black, vine black, to the resins
Of darkness. That is how good a picture
Should be, oil abetting, light disturbing,
Hoisted between two windows like the soul
Of modesty, constantly straightening against them.

But I am agitated less by glass or apertures
Than moisture trapped like a stain or white
Secretion, an old swab I was confident
Had broken down to paste, or was ingrained
In the next meconium, my intent and cherished waste.

Catching Geese

Dreaming is after I decline to sleep
With you, but stay in the depths
Of the bed, winding you round my arm.
If I disappear, it's only to worry you
Into getting the children on their feet,
Or putting a rosary out in the rain
To turn the house gold again, facing
The wall of a church. You're unhappy
At my fern-fisted handshake, I'm unhappy
That my fresh hunger doesn't block your throat
Like a person. Even the sun should be as different
As my soon-to-be-famous blue style from
My letter-perfect rose, a period of wood
Marbleized to promise stone — hot as the close
Of summer's complete scheme in lace-trimmed
White, which, if I wanted to write about,
All I had to do to hold the sentence still
Was paint it on the circumference of a plate,
And every sound of you crying could be heard.

Partly Dedicated to a House

Afraid of the window's glance all blue
And despairing, I press home the crisis
It imposes; and the taste I'd like you
To have found there turns our love
Into the same thirsty act of contemplation.

Not so long ago, words spoken too soon,
Such as 'It really is over', prolonged
Themselves in prearranged silences
Like inert stations on a line. And
Though it was in essence anything but over,
These are the places I now prefer,
The farmyard where we had fallen out
Swept clean and hungrier.

Leave your letter for five hours on a
Blotting-pad to isolate and then add
Which one of us is writing to which,
Expecting an imaginary reply.

Something Like a Wind

Your lips were always a single line of time
Flowing through a single place — day after day,
Like kisses bestowed on both cheeks, they
Fastened the years together, when I would like
To have prised them ever so gently apart.

When you said it had taken us several hours
Less than the normal amount to pass
From one night into the next, I agreed with the bird
That you were ill, how deeply wrong
Were all our movements, like someone waking

With no one in a mixture of morning and lamplight.
I wanted the bird just then, even more than the
Slightly rocking sea, its sound as entirely blue
As if it were a scrap of sky, with something
Like a wind blowing over it. For

The silences immersed between the waves
Were poor streets where women might present themselves
As points of darkness only, things that happen,
Good times — and I intended to watch
The sun kneel down before the mountain.

Sabbath Park

My absolute address is Sabbath Park
And the traditional light blue of its
Paradise Lost room, which I took to be
My mother. Sometimes in the evenings
I would ask, a step not easily taken,
Whether the bird learns to build its nest
Like that — a perfect nest from such
Arthritic wood. My heart was satisfied
Only by the right to be hurt that
Cleans the body like a flow of blood,
So that its pleasure is to have no pleasure,
Or to listen to itself hoarding
Some particularly luminous autumn
Out of all those harmless arctic summers.

Now, after a year misspent on the ragged
Garden side of the door, I put faith
In a less official entrance, the accidental
Oblongs of the windows that I find
Have neither catch nor pulley. Broody
As a seven-months' child, I upset
The obsolete drawing-room that still seems
Affronted by people having just gone,
By astonishing Louisa with my sonnets,
Almost a hostage in the dream
Of her mother's hands — that would leave them
Scattered over their damask sofas after
Some evening party, filled
With the radiance of my fine lawn shirt.

I feel the swaggering beginnings
Of a new poem flaring up, because the house
Is dragging me into its age, the malady
Of fireplaces crammed with flowers, even
On a golden winter Sunday. No matter

How hysterically the clouds swing out,
They may not alter by one drop of rain
The safari of the garden beds, or make
Louisa's dress, with its oyster-coloured overlay
Of moss, kidnap me kindly for a day,
As though a second wife were sleeping
Already in your clothes, the sewn
Lilies near the ground growing downward.

Miss Twelves

The mischief of the sky striking
Our side of the house, that was childhood
Just beginning to shake — the only bit
Of childhood I had left. I could have
Put my finger in the dark before
On most of our handles and spouts, without
Wanting colour to help me, not even
The milky lemon-blue you find
In the seed of wild balsam. It seemed
To me that nothing had been dusted
Since our house was built. I foresaw
How small the hall had grown, such
A slip of a garden! And my wedding
Dress would have loose sleeves with
Light swansdown under them, to show
Why one is so unwilling to let go
What I have heard called 'Sweet
Seventeen' — having felt shy there
Myself, distinct in candlelight.